Writing with Hemingway

A Writer's Exercise Book

Cathy MacHold

Photographs by Kenneth F. MacHold
Cover design by Karen Phillips
Edited by Suzy McMinn & Paul Chollet

Printed in the United States

First Edition 2016

Published by WWH Press

Library of Congress Cataloging-in-Publication Data
Writing with Hemingway, A Writer's Exercise Book
MacHold, Cathy

ISBN-10: 0-9964492-05
ISBN-13: 978-0-9964492-0-5

Retrieve from your mind a creative spirit that moves from your heart onto paper.

Cathy MacHold

Any work of creativity such as an artist's song, a dance, a musical instrument, a paint brush, produce a vision or a sound powerful enough to evoke emotion. A word or sentence can do the same. If properly placed, words stir thoughts and harness pure emotion, drawing a reader into a story. But, how do we get those words onto paper?

The answer might be found, in part, in this beautiful African proverb, "What comes from the lips reaches the ears, what comes from the heart reaches the heart."

An artist, a singer, a dancer or a musician cannot achieve success without discipline. Many hours of practice are necessary. Any art form requires time to perfect it. The same holds true for a writer. A writer must write. A writer must write many things in many ways to achieve a goal as a successful writer. Use this book to practice. Select a page and write. Or, start at the first page and work your way through. You will notice improvements in your work. Over time, you will develop your own writing style as you learn to write from your heart.

Soak in Hemingway information as you complete these exercises. Enjoy photos of a walking tour of Hemingway's northern Michigan. He visited this area each summer from his birth in 1899 until he married Hadley Richardson at Horton Bay in 1921. The photos capture the influences used in his short stories early in his writing career. Other photos include The Hemingway Home in Key West, Florida; Ketchum, Idaho; and the Finca Vigia, Hemingway's home in Cuba. All photos in this book are from my personal Hemingway experiences.

This book is structured for you to write a variety of responses. Use it to your advantage. Some questions intentionally provide a small area in which to write. For other questions more space is available. This is part of the exercise. If you are inspired to write more on a particular topic, then continue writing on an added page. Exercises begin small and work into larger pieces. You will find an essay on page 149 for you to edit and critique. This is another exercise. This is not a diary. Be creative. Free yourself to write honestly.

Cathy MacHold

When Ernest Hemingway was asked for writing tips, he would often respond by suggesting a writer, write the best story as straight as he could.

1. When fear filled you, how did you shake it away? Write it the best and as straight as you can.

This 2014 photo of Potter's Rooming House, located at 602 State Street, is a private residence. A historical marker is located on the property.

2. In the fall of 1919, Ernest Hemingway rented a room in Potter's Rooming House in Petoskey, Michigan. Write a few words about Mrs. Eva Potter, a widow living there with her children, and why it was necessary for her to rent out a room.

3. There is a story within everyone. Tell your story in 59 words.

4. Write about frustration and things that frustrate you as a writer.

5. A compliment can spark joy when given sincerely. Write the compliment you would like to receive.

The Perry Hotel as it appeared in 2014.

6. In 1916, Ernest Hemingway and a friend hiked and camped their way from Oak Park, Illinois to northern Michigan, where they stayed at the Perry Hotel in Petoskey, Michigan. Write a brief story about their adventure.

Hemingway has been quoted as saying that it is good to be tired in one's body and to be tired after making love with whom you loved. That it could fill you up but you might feel empty later.

7. Write about being tired in the body connecting it with whom you love and a possible meaning of feeling empty later.

8. You once rescued a pet. Write about the emotional experience it left with you.

9. While living in Cuba, Hemingway sought out a Castilian-accented Spanish teacher for his fourth wife, Mary Welsh. He felt the accent was easily understood, more so than the Cuban-Spanish accent. Write, incorporating a second language in your story.

Little Traverse Historical Society History Museum was renamed in the 1960s. In Hemingway's time it was called the Pere Marquette Railroad Station. Hemingway traveled between Charlevoix and Petoskey often on this railroad.

10. Write a train-trip experience that would work in a story.

11. As an only child, note your advantage over those who have siblings and how this could work into your character as an interesting part of your story.

_____

_____

_____

_____

_____

_____

_____

_____

12. You impulsively purchased a fly-fishing pole complete with gear. Write that story.

_____

_____

_____

_____

_____

_____

_____

_____

_____

_____

_____

_____

_____

_____

_____

_____

_____

_____

13. You received a letter with disturbing information. Write about your reaction.

14. You recently traveled to a critical location for your story. Write about why this is critical.

15. There is a painting that you often think of. Describe the reasons why you are attracted to it.

Ernest Hemingway once remarked that F. Scott Fitzgerald would change his good stories prior to submission because they would be more salable as magazine stories if he did. Hemingway felt that was "whoring." He felt Fitzgerald was not true to his writing style.

16. What is your impression of this statement? How might this affect the writing style of your story?

17. Write about a trip to the hospital. What happened and how did you feel?

18. Describe your private space and why you value it.

Carnegie Library building in 2014.

19. The Carnegie Library was a favorite haunt of Ernest Hemingway when he lived in Petoskey, Michigan in late 1919. Here, he spoke to the Ladies Aid Society about his recent World War I experience as an ambulance driver for the Italian Red Cross. It was where he met the Connable family who later helped him gain employment as a European correspondent for the Toronto Star newspaper. This was his first big break. Write about the place you haunt. Include your impression of this meeting as opportunity or luck.

20. A character in one of your stories does not cook. How does this play into the story?

21. A particular subject challenges a student character in your short story. Write an example of how you used this in your sketch.

22. Write about a best friend, describing why your story character is endearing.

23. A young driver suddenly slams on the car brakes—for what reason?

24. Write 250 words about a car accident.

25. Write 100 words describing a scary movie.

_____
_____
_____
_____
_____
_____
_____
_____
_____
_____
_____
_____
_____
_____

26. A thought provoking question must be revealed in your story. Elaborate how you will bring it forward.

_____
_____
_____
_____
_____
_____
_____
_____
_____
_____
_____
_____
_____

Hemingway felt bittersweet after completing a story that he thought was very good. He would realize the next day, after re-reading his material, how good it truly was.

27. Your writer has experienced similar feelings. Fill this page with that assessment.

28. Hemingway wrote across varied genres. He worked as a journalist. He wrote fiction, creative nonfiction, poetry, and as a journalist. Select a style to write on this page.

29. Hemingway worked for the Kansas City Star during 1917 and 1918, writing police and emergency room notices. He followed the Star's journalistic style through his career. In 1958, Hemingway told George Plimpton that the 110 rules were a benefit to anyone. He suggested writing short first paragraphs using vigorous English in a positive manner. The Kansas City Star website: www.kansascity.com/entertainment/books/article offers a style sheet that can be downloaded, copied, or printed. Write 500 words using the guidelines.

30. American novelist, poet, and playwright, Gertrude Stein taught Hemingway about "automatic writing." She suggested writing in huge strokes in blue school notebooks. She felt filling pages as quickly as possible, getting out all the free association, puns, and ideas. Hemingway thought of this as short-circuiting and pumping the brain. Use Stein's technique for something you are currently writing.

31. Describe a scene from your story using a technique from one of your favorite authors.

32. Fill this page with the advice you would give at your own funeral, if you could.

Hemingway did not drink after dinner, nor while writing. Perhaps he felt it was good discipline.

33. What disciplines guide you with your writing?

34. Write from the point of view of a daughter recalling a special day spent with her father.

35. Your character must give advice to a child who had just lost a parent. Write about it.

The Grand Rapids and Indiana Railroad Station in Petoskey, Michigan in 2014.

36. The Hemingway family passed through the Grand Rapids and Indiana Railroad Station often when going from Harbor Springs to their Walloon Lake cottage. Ernest used the train station as his model in his novel, *The Torrents of Spring*, set in the Petoskey area. Describe in detail, a location you have considered in your writing.

37. Age shapes a character in a story. Write how age affects your character and the importance of using this in your story. Use an example.

38. Your character acts in a particular manner when no one is watching. Write about it.

39. Your young child character wishes she could do something over again. Write part of that story.

40. A character in your sketch is an octogenarian. He has been asked to speak to a group of graduating seniors. What will he say?

41. You plan to include a traditional family Sunday supper in your story. It is a turning point for your story. Write it here.

42. Hemingway wrote short stories based on people he met. Write about characters who would make memorable impressions based on people you know.

43. Write honestly about the length your character goes to renew a lost friendship.

44. The child in your story has given a compliment to her mother. It was surprising and beautiful. Write this part of your story.

45. The things that come easiest to you tell a great story. Write an example of a beginning, middle and ending of something that comes easy.

_____
_____
_____
_____
_____
_____
_____
_____
_____
_____
_____
_____

46. A character in your story must keep a secret, but Jennifer gets in the way. Write about this.

_____
_____
_____
_____
_____
_____
_____
_____
_____
_____
_____
_____
_____
_____

Hemingway enjoyed visiting Gertrude Stein's residence during his Paris years. He enjoyed her paintings, conversations, and the stories from other people who visited her residence. He felt it was important to be open-minded in his thinking and, perhaps, not associating his work during these experiences. He wanted his subconscious to work at the same time as listening to others completely.

47. Write about awareness of a character and how thoughts are collected both consciously and subconsciously.

48. In your story, something nudges your character's memory forward. Write about it.

49. Write about an influential person.

50. The time traveler in your story explains the reason for going back in time. What is it?

_____

_____

_____

_____

_____

_____

_____

_____

_____

_____

_____

51. A person in your story weighs twenty pounds less than yesterday. How did that happen?

_____

_____

_____

_____

_____

_____

_____

_____

_____

_____

_____

_____

_____

52. Your love story has a female character receiving red roses on Valentine's Day from three different people. Write about it.

_____

_____

_____

_____

_____

_____

_____

_____

_____

_____

_____

_____

53. In your latest short story your obsessed character, who has just moved, brought along a house plant that is forty years old. Tell the story.

_____

_____

_____

_____

_____

_____

_____

_____

_____

_____

_____

_____

_____

54. You hold a crazy-busy day in your memory. It is a story that must be told. Write that short story.

55. You are unable to sleep. Get up and write about what?

City Park Grill
Petoskey, Michigan
2014

56. The Annex was a popular place for Hemingway to enjoy playing billiards and watching bare-knuckle boxing matches in a nearby park. It served as inspiration for the saloon in Hemingway's story, *A Man of the World*. Today it is known as City Park Grill. Write about a place as inspiration in your story.

57. Through history, clothes have evolved as costumes. Explain how you have used the clothes of a character in one of your stories.

58. Money plays a significate role in one of your stories. Write what it means.

59. Write about what you are most conscientious about.

60. You think it is silly when people ask you what your favorite color is but when you look around your living environment, you notice a common color. What color is it and how does that affect you?

61. Halloween is your favorite time to celebrate. What do you enjoy most about wearing a costume? How will you work a significate costume into your story?

_____

_____

_____

_____

_____

_____

_____

_____

_____

62. Write about a contest you won and why it was important.

_____

_____

_____

_____

_____

_____

_____

_____

_____

_____

_____

_____

_____

_____

_____

_____

_____

63. Write about the longest stretch of time you have been away from home.

64. You do not smoke marijuana but have enjoyed trying it in the past. Write of your experience in obtaining it.

65. When was the lie better than the truth? Use it in a short tale.

66. You told your parents a secret that you swore to a sibling not to tell. What is that story?

67. Create a short story in this space about how you trained your dog to stay in the yard without a fence.

You have written what you consider to be an excellent piece of work. But, your editor suggests it is "inaccroachable." Gertrude Stein used this word in an explanation to Hemingway. Her meaning is it is like a picture that cannot be hung just anywhere. Nobody would buy it if they could not hang it.

68. This advice from Gertrude Stein to Hemingway means what to you?

69. Your mother worked while you were growing up. You came home from school to an empty house. Write some of those memories.

70. As a runner, you were disciplined to stay in shape and eat healthy. What was your routine?

71. Write of a time when you were your dirtiest and what you remember about that time.

72. Write about the circumstances of a time when you discovered that you were a jealous person. Include how you acted in that situation.

McCarthy's Barber Shop was once located in this building in Petoskey, Michigan.

73. McCarthy's Barber Shop was once located in this building. It was not only a barber shop but also the location of a public bath in the building's basement. In the fall of 1919, young Hemingway would enjoy a shave or a haircut and the patrons banter about fishing and politics. McCarthy's Barber Shop is referred to by name in Hemingway's novel, *The Torrents of Spring*. Imagine banter from a barber shop or hair salon and write about it.

74. Write about a stranger who haunts your heart. Write honest and true. Do not leave anything out.

75. What made a perfect day so?

76. The words of your favorite song bring emotion and heart-felt feeling forward. Write about the song.

77. Though you enjoy many talents of your own, what talent do you wish for?

78. You made your mother very angry. Write about that time.

79. Describe an endearing moment with your mother when you felt completely connected and loved.

80. You are one of the first astronauts landing on Mars. Why were you selected over others?

81. What is the strangest sight you have witnessed in a cross walk?

82. When you get into bed at night, what are the first thoughts moving through your mind?

_____
_____
_____
_____
_____
_____
_____
_____
_____
_____
_____
_____

83. You prepared a wonderful meal. The memory of it lingers on your taste buds. Write that story.

_____
_____
_____
_____
_____
_____
_____
_____
_____
_____
_____
_____
_____
_____
_____
_____

84. You enjoyed a memorable meal prepared by someone other than you. Write that story.

85. You returned from a trip to Bordeaux, France with a fine selection of wines. You decided not to share them with guests. Why?

86. A stranger mistook you for someone else. Who? What happened next?

87. You are not bothered that you tipped the scale ten pounds more this morning than a week ago. Write the circumstances.

Non-conceited writers have a shyness about them when they have completed something special and fine. This paraphrased quote is from *The Moveable Feast*.

88. Hemingway was referring to F. Scott Fitzgerald in his quote about humility. Write about humility and how it is an advantage or disadvantage for you as a writer.

89. You made a sacrifice which benefited someone else. Write about it.

90. Someone made a sacrifice that benefited you. Write about the experience.

91. As a child, you loved your babysitter like a mother and treated her so. Later she betrayed you.
How?

92. Wild turkeys invaded your pristine vineyard. Write an action story of how you chased them away.

93. Write a paragraph explaining why you named all your dogs with the same name.

94. Write about a time when you felt prideful.

95. Immediately, you regretted what you said. What was it? Write the story.

96. There is a recessed story of shame. Write about it.

97. Your newest story includes a character who values privacy above all else. Tell us about this character.

98. Write a paragraph about love.

99. Complete this: Barely could I look him in the eyes for I...

100. Explain why Mrs. Jones stayed in bed for two years then decided it was time to get up again.

101. Your father decided that boarding school was the best option for your education. Write a story of that experience.

102. You walked past it every day for many years, then saw it for the first time. Write the story.

103. Write the meaning of living in a bubble and why it is a good choice.

104. In your story, your spouse wants a recreational vehicle to use in retirement. You do not. How is this resolved in your story?

105. After thirty years of marriage, the main character of your story discovers that his spouse cheated on him fifteen years prior. What are the plot turns that brought this forward in your story?

106. A character, in a funny story you are writing decides to keep a birthday gift bought for another. Your character attends the party without the gift and tells others what he did. Write the funny parts.

_____
_____
_____
_____
_____
_____
_____
_____
_____
_____
_____
_____
_____
_____

107. Write 400 words maximum about a homecoming experience.

_____
_____
_____
_____
_____
_____
_____
_____
_____
_____

Hemingway would study a particular Cezanne painting and try to learn, from the simplicity of the art, how to write stories with dimension, through simplicity. He would try and learn but felt he was not yet articulate enough to explain it to anyone. He even thought that the discovery could be a secret.

108. Imagine standing in front of a famous painting. You are looking for structure for your writing. Write about the artist, the painting, and what you learned.

109. The child in front of you at the check-out counter slipped a candy bar into his mother's bag without her or the checker noticing. Write your reaction.

110. Your character ate part of the newly-purchased birthday cake he was taking home for his daughter's birthday. How did you explain away this action in your story?

Jesperson's Restaurant
312 Howard Street
Petoskey, Michigan
2014

111. Jesperson's Restaurant in Petoskey claims to be Hemingway's favorite hangout. The long lunch counter was used for scenes in his story, *The Killers*, and in his novel *The Torrents of Spring*. Visualize customers patronizing Jesperson's during 1919, then write about them in your short story.

112. There are many reasons why it happened. But, now it has gone on for so long that you think you would sound crazy when explaining it. The truth is you have stashed over one million dollars, wrapped in bundles, in your bedroom closet. Write the rest of this story.

113. Write 100 words explaining the reason your character did not pick up the ringing phone.

114. You awoke sweating from a fitful night of sleep. Write about the experience.

115. You are assigned to write a war story. Write from your point of view.

116. Your female character is babysitting her young nephew. While shopping, she suddenly notices that he is missing. Write the story.

117. In a dramatic fiction story you've been writing, while kayaking in Lake Tahoe, your main character finds a body floating face up in the water. Most drowning victims are found face down. Write a section of the story.

118. In the middle of the night someone pounded at your front door, frantically yelling, "Let me in, let me in, help me." What did you do?

119. Sitting in class, you look out the window and your mind wanders. Where?

120. Recall a sad feeling then write about it.

121. Why does that clothing item still hang in your closet with the price tag on it?

122. What sport do you deeply wish to play professionally?

123. You never thought it could happen to you, but then it did. Write about it.

124. Write about the biggest surprise of your life.

125. What celebrity would play you in a movie about an event in your life? Write the story.

Hemingway believed in living life fully and writing about what he knew. He wrote about subjects that were new and interesting to a large audience. This became the backdrop for much of his work. He wrote stories of war, big game hunting, bull fighting, and boxing. His themes included love, death, and betrayal. He thought of this as writing the truest one could write.

126. Write the truest you can, using a theme, and backdrop from the above statement.

127. You saw something then later realized you should have reported it to the police. Now is your chance to come clean.

128. Your biggest surge of confidence came from what?

129. What inspires you?

130. You looked into the prettiest eyes you have ever seen. Describe the effect on you.

131. You felt emotional opposites simultaneously. Describe the experience.

132. Your character is a sibling. She said something in your story conversation that took the protagonist to a forgotten place. Where was it and why was it lodged so far back in memory?

133. The main character in your story shared a guarded secret with her best friend. Later, she discovered her friend discussed it with her daughter. Write more of the story.

134. A character in your story has enjoyed many wonderful things in life. So many, in fact, that he or she has lost sight of joy. Write how you would bring joy back to your character.

135. As a writer, you see how politics are played out in the movies. Write a few sentences showing how your character's vote is counted.

136. Write a lengthy description of how you look today.

137. What was the last subject of a story you wrote about and what made it important?

138. Your story section is under pressure to meet a deadline. Write about it.

Boat dock at
Walloon Lake, Michigan
2014

139. Walloon Lake is six miles from the Hemingway family's summer cabin called Windemere, in northern Michigan. Nearby is Horton Bay where in 1929, Ernest Hemingway married Hadley Richardson. Hemingway was inspired by many people from this area. Some served as models for characters in his short stories and novels. Write two pages from a summer vacation experience and the people whose character inspired you.

140. Hemingway's first published piece was written for his school newspaper, The Trapeze, about a local musical performance. Write a review for a local high school musical performance.

141. The phrase "lost generation" was popularized by Hemingway in his publication of *The Sun Also Rises*. Write your interpretation of the meaning of "lost generation?"

Both Hadley Richardson's father and Ernest Hemingway's father committed suicide. Only after the death of his father did Ernest realize how Hadley may have felt about her father's death in 1903. Ernest later commented, "I'll probably go the same way."

142. Write your thoughts on suicide and Hemingway's statement.

Ernest Hemingway lived in Cuba for 30 years. Cubans consider Hemingway as their personal writer. One can find many memorials for Hemingway throughout the country. In Old Havana, the Hotel Ambos Mundos maintains room 511 as a Hemingway museum. The furniture belongs to the hotel but the possessions came from the Finca Vigia, Hemingway's home in Cuba.

143. There is a story in how Hemingway's possessions ended up as a memorial in room 511 of the Hotel Ambos Mundos. Tell it.

144. Hemingway enjoyed a meal of fish. He would provide his favorite recipes to local bars and restaurants in Cuba and, sometimes the catch. Describe a memorable meal in great detail.

145. Music moves emotion through movies but how is music expressed in books? Write a piece of your story working music into it.

146. Hearing a song has the power to return you to the place where you first heard it. What song takes your reader to what place?

147. Write an example of the September 11, 2001 experience into your story.

148. Write circumstances that resulted in sleepless nights for a long period.

149. A compromise ended favorably in your story. It was not easily accomplished. Explain.

150. Write about the unfinished business in your story that changes the ending.

151. Adriana's scar faintly ropes from the left side of her 12-year old face, down under her ear, ending near the top of her shoulder. Write the rest of the story.

152. Hemingway's mentors included writer Gertrude Stein, poet Ezra Pound, and writer James Joyce, among others. Identify your mentors. Include examples of their influence in your writing.

153. The foundation style of Hemingway's writing uses short sentences, short first paragraphs with vigorous, positive English. Write a short story using these guidelines on the next 1 ½ pages.

154. Hemingway referred to his writing style as using the iceberg theory: the facts float about the water, the supporting structure and symbolisms operate out of sight. With this in mind, write a short story completing this page.

155. The son in your story makes more money than his father, Michael. Michael is happy for him but sees that he fits into a stupid-rich generation, spending money frivolously. Michael is from the Great Depression era and does not approve. Write the letter he will give to his son addressing this issue.

156. Hemingway used autobiographical detail as a framing device about life. This writing technique worked in many of his short stories. Try writing a short story using this technique.

On the cover of this workbook is a photo of Hemingway's Corona No. 3 typewriter. The photo was taken by Ken MacHold at the Finca Vigia in San Francisco de Paula, Havana, Cuba. Hemingway owned many typewriters in his lifetime. His first wife, Hadley, gave him this one for his 23rd birthday in 1922.

157. Describe the tools, habits, smells, and setting of your workspace. Write it into a few paragraphs.

158. Write about close relatives and what makes their relationships endearing.

159. As a successful writer, it is possible for you to live anywhere in the world. Write the story of why you live where you live.

160. Write the struggle of landing a marlin like Hemingway did.

161. The twenty-nine-year-old protagonist in your story is brooding over the end of his marriage. Tell the story of his anguish.

162. Hemingway met pretty, Adriana Ivancich, a juene fille bien élevée, just shy of nineteen in Italy. He became infatuated with Adriana and she with him though their relationship was called platonic. Later Adriana designed the cover art for two of Hemingway's books, *The Old Man and the Sea,* and *Across the River and Into the Trees.* Tell a version of how this happened.

163. Your character is haunted by something from the past that she wanted and did not get. Write about it.

164. In the same story as above, a color brings what memory back to your character? Tell that piece.

165. The last third of your book is a chapter about the tragic death of a favorite pet. Write about it.

166. In his short story, *The Short Happy Life of Francis Macomber,* Hemingway describes boy-men. This phrase is fairly common today as Jimmy Fallon has used the phrase on the Tonight Show. Hemingway was known for his manly pursuits. Write a boy-men piece into your story capturing your definition of the phrase.

167. There is a vacant lot for sale in the neighborhood where you live. You are planning to work this into a scene in your story. Write it.

168. You have been asked to be a guest on a radio talk show to discuss your book. What will you talk about?

169. You have decided to use your first kiss experience in your next short story. What will you write?

170. Write the part in your story about an impulsive thing that got your character into trouble.

171. A child in your story knows he could be better at something if he put work into it but he doesn't. Write a few paragraphs about the work missing from the story.

172. Your latest story is about a writer who owns 1,200 books. What is the best part of his story?

173. Your story is being filmed as a movie. A clunky old 1966 Karmann Ghia is in one scene. Tell the story.

174. It has been a long time since your protagonist last saw her friend, Kristen. They parted on bad terms, and now Kristen wants to explain why she has stayed away. Tell the story.

175. Countless bars in Havana, Key West, Ketchum, and Petoskey offer cocktails named in your honor. Write how you feel about this.

176. Lovers in your story cannot agree on a tropical beach vacation or a winter ski trip. Write how it ends.

177. Melissa was thrilled that her mother allowed her to ride the Ferris wheel. Then, it stopped with her on top. What happens next?

In the book, *The Paris Wife,* Paula McLain writes about Hadley. Hadley, as the main character, is talking about the things Hemingway was learning from his early mentor, Gertrude Stein. Gertrude began to influence his style, particularly the habit she had of naming and repeating specific objects, places, and people. Stein did not try to find variation, but revealed how any word took on a striking power when used again and again. During this period, Hemingway was writing a series of short stories. Hadley saw how Hemingway was applying Stein's technique. The simplest language and things---lake, trout, log, boat---gave his work a very distilled and almost mythic feel.

178. This was called automatic writing. Try this approach, creating something new on this page.

Hemingway referred to northern Michigan essential places; Horton Bay, Petoskey, Walloon Lake, Charlevoix, and used these for backdrops in his Nick Adams stories. This was a clever way of connecting solutions for a series of short stories.

179. Write an outline on the following pages. Use automatic writing to brainstorm a series of short story ideas set in a backdrop location.

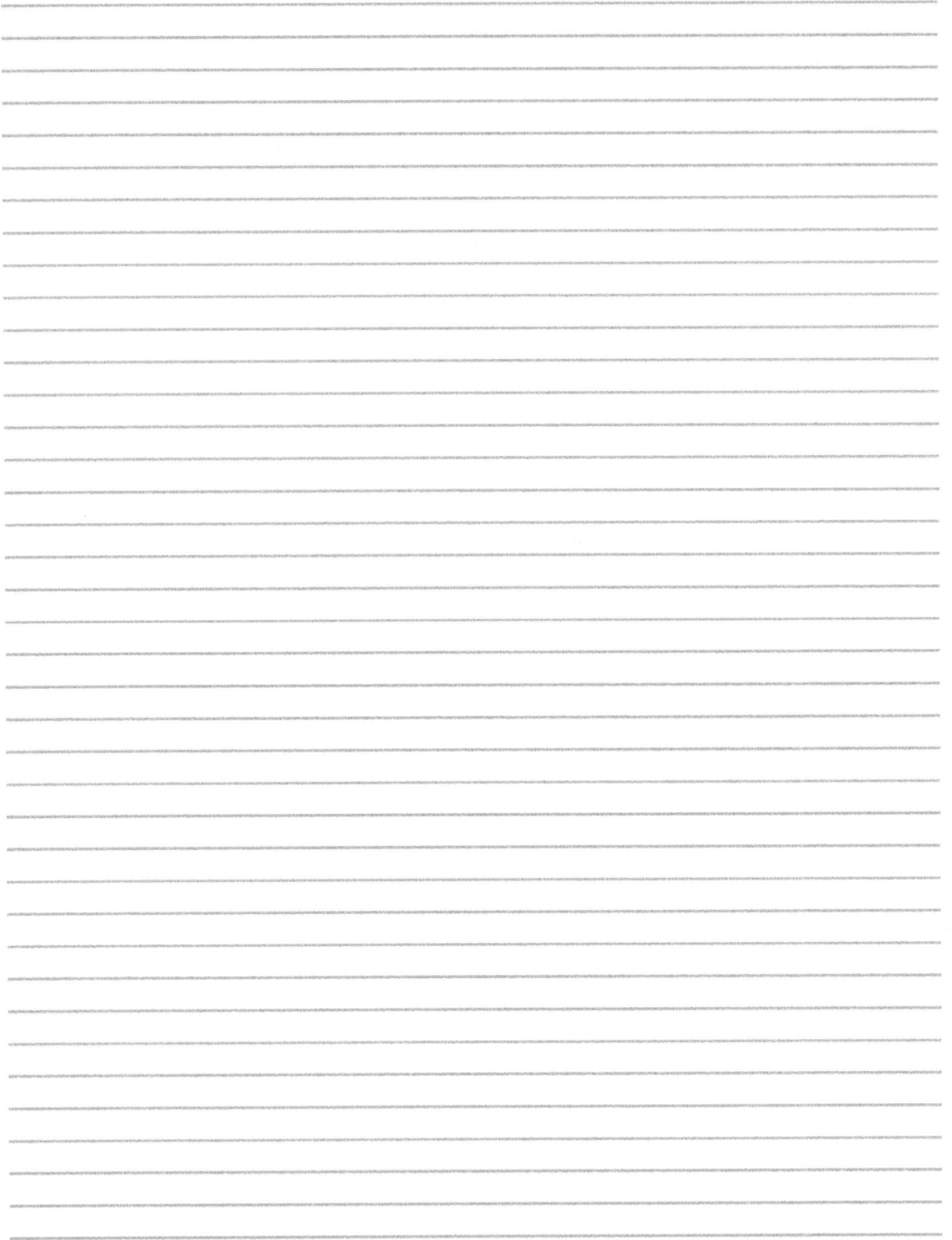

Ernest Hemingway made many hair references in his stories. He described how Gertrude Stein looked like a northern Italian peasant woman who piled her alive, emigrant hair high and wrapped it around her head. Gertrude later bobbed her hair and taught Ernest how to cut Hadley's hair.

180. Write an example of how you might use hair to draw emotion into a story.

A Moveable Feast was written as a memoir in 1959 from forgotten material stored in trunks since 1928. But, in an earlier time, 1922, Hemingway was very upset at Hadley when his manuscripts were stolen from her care as she traveled to meet him in Paris. The irony here is both a beginning and an ending.

181. Write irony into a story here.

182. Create a situation in a story where your character is tempted with a questionable offer. Write about the reaction as you tell the story.

183. The world of writing includes story telling.   If you belong to a writing group, you might read your material for critique. Write a story, reading it to yourself several times and then read it to your critique group.

_____
_____
_____
_____
_____
_____
_____
_____
_____
_____
_____
_____

184. You've been asked by the local paper to report a vehicular accident in the mountains. Write that here.

_____
_____
_____
_____
_____
_____
_____
_____
_____
_____
_____
_____
_____

Writers have words stirring in their mind. If they awake you or disturb you in any way, you must put those words into writing. They need to be sifted, shaped, and splashed onto paper. Don't lose them by waiting for tomorrow.

185. Write some of the story ideas that wake you in your sleep or disturb your thoughts.

Hemingway historical
marker at Walloon Lake
in northern Michigan.

186. From Petoskey, Michigan, go southeast of Horton Bay on the Boyne City Charlevoix Road for approximately one mile, turn due east onto Sumner Road and follow it to the end. This is where you will see the Hemingway historical marker and Walloon Lake public access marker. It did not exist in Hemingway's time but since he spent the summers of his youth there, he knew the area well. Write an adventure from a remembered summer, basing it here at Walloon Lake.

187. A woman sat in the corner drinking, observing lives of other patrons. Near closing, she watched the bartender clean, wipe and refill. Then, an old man entered, his clothes, shabby and torn.
"Hey, let me taste the day." he said.
 Without looking up, the bartender poured the drippings from the shot mats into a glass.
"Here you go Max." Write the story.

188. A young child has inspired you. Write the story.

189. Your story includes a woman, who at 50, decided to get a makeover. Write this part of the story.

Hemingway learned to see the female point of view from novelist and poet, James Joyce. He learned that characters could become both male and female. He learned that a woman's hair stimulated erotic imagination. This was very different from the pre-Raphaelite hair of his mother or his memories of his sisters drying their hair in the sun. In *The Paris Wife*, Paula McLain writes of Hemingway and Hadley cutting their hair the same, becoming the same person. I am you, you are me.

190. Write a story with characters who are both male and female. Include a hair scene.

191. A character in your story thinks of himself as a man of reason in a world filled with superstition. Explain how this character finds a logical explanation for a strange occurrence in your story.

Though Hemingway was a tough character, it was often difficult for him to sift through all the critics of his work. Once he submitted work to his agent, he became impatient awaiting a reply. He sometimes sent telegrams several times a day, nearly begging for information.

192. Visualize Hemingway as your character. He lives in Cuba where he is fairly isolated. He must rely on telegrams for most of his communication. Write a story using this premise.

193. Ernest Hemingway suffered many life-threatening injuries during his lifetime. He was seriously injured during World War I. He volunteered as an ambulance driver in Italy in 1918. Write a story in first person about war and how war has affected you.

194. In 1928, Hemingway pulled a skylight down thinking it was the toilet chain. It caused a severe head injury. Write about the experience as though it happened to you. Build on each sentence with drama.

195. Much of Hemingway's material for his writing was based on themes of love, war, wilderness, and loss. They are recurring themes in American literature. Use this page to set up a dramatic story. Place action where you feel it will support the theme you are writing about.

In the book *Ernest Hemingway* by Carlos Baker, Baker writes of a time in late December of 1948 when Hemingway met Adriana Ivancich. Ernest and Mary Hemingway were traveling in Venice. Adriana tagged along with a group of Italian friends for a duck hunting excursion. Later, Adriana, a little bruised by the shooting, sat by an open fire drying her hair. She chatted with Hemingway. In a moment of gallantry, Hemingway retrieved the comb from his pocket, broke it in half and gave Adriana the other half. *Across the River and Into the Trees* is a novel by Hemingway. He used Adriana as Renata, a character in the story. They continued a platonic relationship until 1951. During that year Hemingway wrote *The Old Man and the Sea*.

196. Write a short story about a platonic relationship.

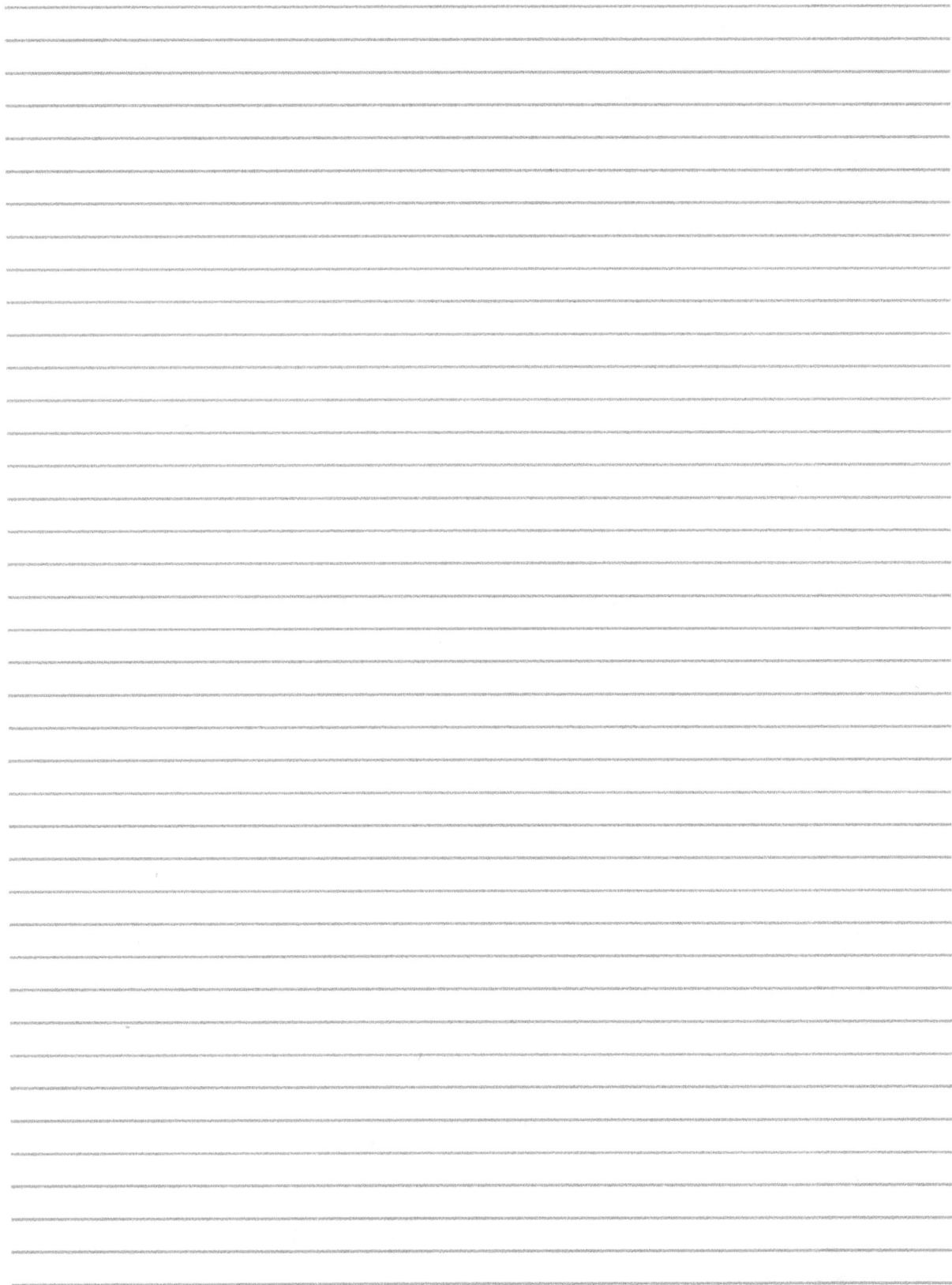

197. Use narratives to develop an experience kayaking on a river when suddenly, a strong current overturns the kayak.

198. Your story is about a woman who relinquished her out-of-wedlock child forty years ago. She is writing a letter full of hope in the rare chance her adult child will make contact with her. Write the letter.

Many books, articles, and stories have been written about the women in Hemingway's life including the tragic suicides in their family. Ernest Hemingway lost his father, Clarence; a brother, Leicester; a sister, Ursula; his third wife Martha; his son Gregory; and his granddaughter, Margaux. His muse, Adriana, hanged herself from a tree in her yard.

199. You have been given an assignment to write about the suicides noted above for a magazine. You are limited to 800 words.

This two-sided Hemingway historical marker is located near Walloon Village, in Melrose Township Park on Walloon Lake in Michigan.

200. Ernest Hemingway's family owned a cabin on Walloon Lake in northern Michigan. Hemingway wrote a series of short stories featuring a character named Nick Adams, set in this area. Today, a historical marker honors Hemingway. The historical marker was inaugurated June 2012, fifty-one years after his death. Write a story of what it might feel like to be honored by the town who inspired your early writing.

201. Develop a short story about a surprise party.

202. Write about a trip to the animal shelter. Include why you selected a dog.

203. A character in your story started a fire. Write about it.

204. While in a dental chair, your character experiences a memorable fantasy. Write the story.

205. Your book includes a cooking scene where a meatloaf is being prepared. It will later be served at a pot luck. Write that story section.

Hemingway's boat, Pilar, was custom built by the Wheeler Ship Yard in New York. In 1934, the cost was about $8000.00. That is the same amount Pauline Pfeiffer's uncle paid for the Hemingway home in Key West, Florida.

206. Write an adventure story of taking ownership of the boat in New York and motoring it home to Key West.

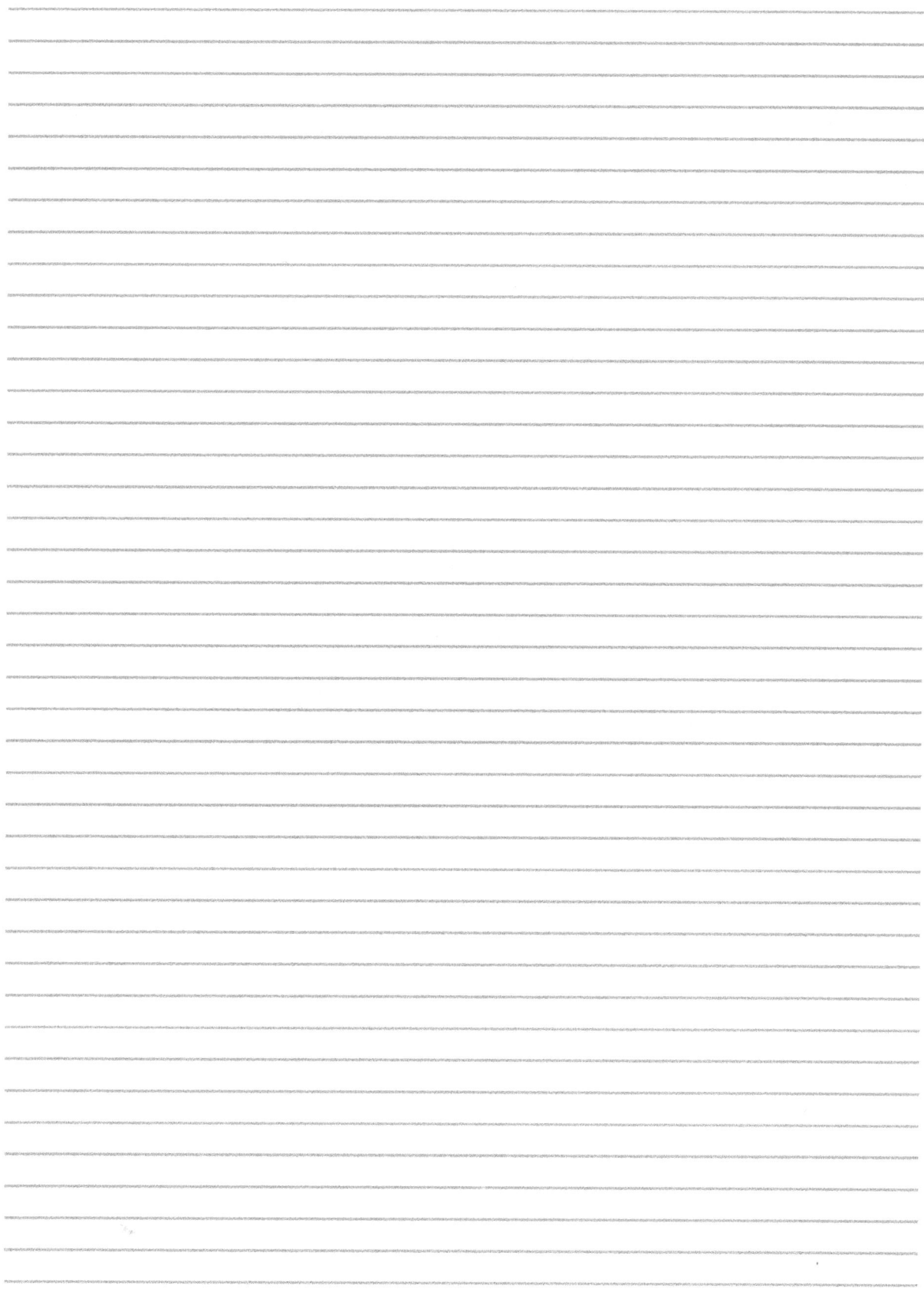

207. In 1930, Hemingway broke his arm in a car accident. He was hospitalized for seven weeks to help heal the damage to his writing hand. Imagine this experience and write about it.

208. Some critics of Hemingway's work suggested that his stories were male-centric of masculine pursuits. Frame a story using this suggestion.

209. Hemingway became enamored with a dozen or more cats when he lived both in Key West and in Cuba. But, during his Paris years, he was appalled when a friend allowed cats to eat from a table. Write a piece about this change and the possible reasons behind it.

210. In 1933, while on safari in the Serengeti, Hemingway contracted amoebic dysentery that caused a prolapsed intestine. Imagine what his wife, Pauline, did to help nurse him back to health. Put into words, her experience.

Edit the following story *The Hemingway Experience*

A warm fall day, along a trail on Big Wood River in Ketchum, Idaho, is about as peaceful and beautiful as a day can be. The glowing shades of yellow seem to change color before your eyes. You can watch leaves from the cottonwoods drift, some falling to the ground, some into the currents of the river. When the air is fresh and quiet, it is best to sit on a log or on the bank where you can observe the changing season. This is the setting for the maximum Hemingway experience in Ketchum.

In the fall of 1939, Gene Van Guilder, a publicist for the new Sun Valley Resort, invited Ernest Hemingway to stay as a guest in the lodge. Van Guilder felt that Hemingway's presence would bring wanted attention to the first destination winter-ski resort in the United States. Though Hemingway felt he might be exploited, he cautiously accepted Van Guilder's offer and with it, one of the most luxurious rooms, Suite 206. This is where he stayed for many seasons to come. Van Guilder and Hemingway grew to be friends through their shared enjoyment of hunting ducks, shooting game birds, and exploring the beautiful country around Ketchum.

Gene was a handsome talented horseman and hunter. He wore western clothes. On a silver-studded saddle he rode his horse. Gene's young life was tragically cut short in late fall of the same year. While duck hunting from a canoe, he was killed by a shotgun carelessly handed to him by one of his fellow hunters. What is remember best from this sad story is the eulogy, in part, delivered by Hemingway:

Best of all he loved the Fall

The leaves yellow on the cottonwoods

Leaves floating on the trout streams and above the hills

The high blue windless skies

Now he will be a part of them forever.

The prose written by Hemingway in 1936 is engraved on The Hemingway Memorial, dedicated in 1966, twenty-five years after it was composed. A sculpture of Hemingway overlooks Trail Creek, 1.5 miles from Sun Valley Lodge.

The journey through the Sierra Nevada is beautiful. The yellows, reds, and orange colors become more spectacular as you near Idaho. Your experience might include a visit to Hemingway's grave, a peek of the Hemingway home, and a photo of the Hemingway Memorial. A walking tour through the town of Ketchum would not be complete without visiting Casino Bar, Sawtooth Club, Whiskey Jacques, or the Pioneer Club; a few of Hemingway's haunts. All adorn their walls with photos of Hemingway. Employees will share a tale or two when asked. The restaurant, Michel's Christiania, is where Hemingway often enjoyed dinner with his wife, Mary. Employees will point out the corner table where Hemingway enjoyed a steak dinner the evening before his suicide on July 2, 1961.

Ketchum is a very small community, population 3,873. It is sprinkled with vacation homes, small businesses and wonderful restaurants. The Ketchum Cemetery is situated between the two main access roads to Sun Valley, Saddle Road to the north and Sun Valley Road to the south. The Sun Valley Lodge is located slightly northeast of town by a few miles.

Sun Valley Lodge reopened on June 15, 2015, following an extensive renovation project. Beautifully framed photographs of Hemingway, Marilyn Monroe, Sonia Henie, Gary Cooper, and John Wayne are displayed along the lobby walls. Suite 206 is where Hemingway worked on *For Whom the Bell Tolls.* It's where he stayed with Martha Gellhorn. Following the renovation, Suite 206 was renamed Suite 228, the Hemingway Suite.

The Community Library is entwined with Hemingway's legacy. Mary and Ernest Hemingway were founding members when its doors opened as a privately funded public library in 1955. The library maintains a large Hemingway collection of oral histories by locals who knew him, original correspondence from Hemingway to Sun Valley locals, signed first edition books, and a full collection of his work. A visit to the library provides a literary look at Hemingway's impact and accomplishments, which remain relevant today.

The Sun Valley Gun Club, another Hemingway haunt, offers trap shooting lessons. You might experience holding a 20-gauge shotgun close to your cheek, nestled into your shoulder. When you align the barrel with the bead at your target for the first time, you will not be prepared for the weight, the sound nor the lightness of ease when pulling the trigger. You can shoot 25 rounds into the White Clouds Mountain Range using environmentally friendly trap targets launched from a single house. It is truly a blast.

Fly fishing lessons are available from one of several outfitters for a nominal fee. After an hour or two learning the basic techniques of fly fishing, you will feel a tingle of excitement when your instructor tells you that you are ready for the river. Then, careful not to snag the fishing pole on the cottonwood trees, you finally enter the stream. Surrounded by colors with the sun on your back, you become settled, peaceful, and one with the fall season. It is here that you'll understand Hemingway's enjoyment of sport fishing. It is also here that you can work your way up Big Wood for a peek at the Hemingway home.

Following her death in 1986, Mary Hemingway bequeathed her home to The Nature Conservancy in Idaho. On August 11, 2015, the conservancy announced that the 14-acre property had been listed in the National Register of Historic Places with "national significance" designation. But, future plans won't change access to the Hemingway home by their invitation-only policy. The home is very hard to find. The Hemingway's purchased the furnished home in 1959. They owned it briefly before his death in 1961. Mary kept the home another 25 years. Hemingway worked on *The Garden of Eden,* editing and rewriting the yet named *A Moveable Feast.*

The best time to visit the small, well-kept Ketchum Cemetery is in the privacy of the early morning light. You will easily find the four tall pine trees that stand over the simple graves of Mary Welsh Hemingway and Ernest Miller Hemingway. Visitors often leave coins, notes, or a bottle of booze for Hemingway. You might be caught off-guard when you visit his gravesite. Even in death, Hemingway produces powerful emotions.

Before your Hemingway experience ends, you might explore the *Ernest Hemingway in Idaho* walking tour. The tour begins at the Sun Valley Museum of History located in the Ketchum Forest Service Park. The museum contains exhibits on local history, ski heritage, and a dedicated "Hemingway in Idaho" exhibit. There are nine other stops as you make your way around Ketchum and Sun Valley. The Ketchum Korral was originally named the MacDonald Cabins when Hemingway first stayed there in 1946. The last stop, Silver Creek Preserve, was one of Hemingway's favorite places to fish. The small town of Hailey is 12 miles south of Ketchum, and is, ironically, where poet Ezra Pound was born. Hemingway first met Pound in Paris as you'll remember from *The Moveable Feast*.

After spending a few days experiencing Hemingway's life in Ketchum, it is easy to understand why he loved the fall season. His presence is everywhere.

211. Critique this essay.

Hemingway wrote a story called *Out of Season*, omitting a part he felt would actually strengthen the story. He wanted people to feel something more than they understood. Hemingway was known for changing how literature was written.

212. Write a story omitting a part that might achieve the goal of strengthening your story.

213. While in London in 1945, Hemingway was hospitalized with a head injury as the result of an automobile accident. In another accident, he injured his knee. At the time, he was married to Martha Gellhorn, his third wife. Both were accomplished war correspondents. Write a scenario about a competitive married couple. Include how these accidents might have happened.

Catwalk to the study at Hemingway's home in Key West, Florida.

214. This catwalk works its way around Hemingway's home in Florida, leading to the gardens and pool house where he would write. Many cats, descendants of the nearly 50 cats who lived during Hemingway's time, continue to make their home here. Write an imagined life with 50 cats to care for.

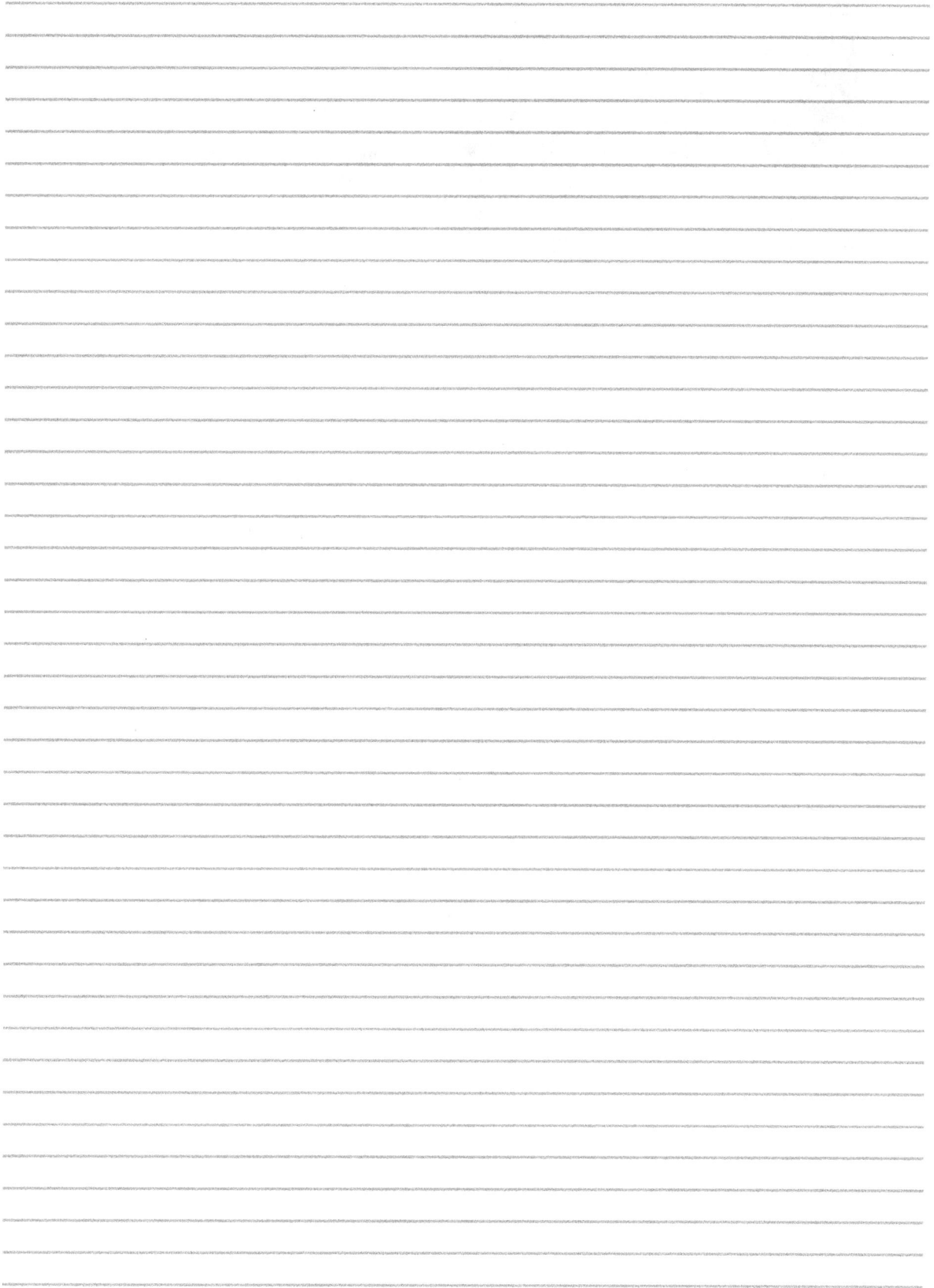

**The Hemingway home
Key West, Florida**

215. Hemingway's home in Key West continues to be one of the most popular tourist attractions in Key West. It was built in 1852 from excavated limestone found in the ground beneath the structure. Having survived many hurricanes, the home was constructed to last. In 1968, the home was registered as a National Historic Landmark. Write an imagined story of the building of this home.

Hemingway's bookcase at his Key West home.

216. This bookcase is located along a hallway wall in Hemingway's Key West home. You might find books by Stephen Crane, Gustave Flaubert, James Joyce, Somerset Maugham, Leo Tolstoy, and others in this collection. A character in your story collects first editions. This is a significate piece of information for your plot. Write a section showing how this plays a role in your story.

217. Between 1955 and 1956, Hemingway was bedridden and told to stop drinking. He was treated for high blood pressure, liver disease, and arteriosclerosis. During this period, he began writing *A Moveable Feast,* a memoir of his early years in Paris. He likely wrote it in pencil because he believed that you get another chance to improve what you have written by first using a pencil. Use a pencil and write a story of your early years.

"How simple the writing of literature would be if it were only necessary to write in another way what has been well-written. It is because we have had such great writers in the past that a writer is driven far out past where he can go, out to where no one can help him." Ernest Hemingway in his Nobel prize acceptance speech.

218. In 1954, Ernest Hemingway was awarded the Nobel Prize for *The Old Man and the Sea*. He was still recovering from two successive plane crashes that left him in pain. He was in bad health and was unable to travel to Stockholm to receive the award. He believed *The Old Man and the Sea* was his best work. It would be his last work published during his lifetime. For a writer, a Nobel Prize is the best success you could achieve. Write an invented meeting with Hemingway and what you would say to him.

Finca Vigia, San Francisco de Paula,
Havana, Cuba

219. Ernest Hemingway lived with his third wife, Martha Gellhorn, in Finca Vigia between 1939 and 1945. Following their divorce, Ernest and Mary Welsh lived at the Finca. Hemingway wrote *For Whom the Bell Tolls* and *The Old Man and the Sea* in a tower located on the property. In the first half of 1961, Hemingway left Cuba to be treated in the United States for severe depression. Following the Bay of Pigs invasion in April of that year, the Hemingways could not return to Cuba. Some of their personal property including manuscripts, were deposited in a vault in Havana. Write a dramatic 700-word story of your attempt to collect items following the confiscation of your property in a political cold war.

Corona No. 3 typewriter owned by Ernest Hemingway on display in his writing studio at the Finca Vigia in Cuba.

220. Hemingway declared this typewriter to be the only psychiatrist he would ever submit to. Imagine a story typed from Hemingway's point of view, on this Corona.

The Hemingway home in Ketchum, Idaho.

221. Ketchum, Idaho was Hemingway's last home. This is where Ernest and his fourth wife of fifteen years, Mary Welsh Hemingway, moved in late 1959. Ernest was nineteen days from his 62nd birthday. The depression which had plagued him during his life seemed to worsen. He unwillingly underwent shock treatments for depression. On July 2, 1961, Ernest walked past Mary's bedroom where she was still asleep, walked into the kitchen taking the keys from the window sill, and walked down to the cellar where his guns were locked in a storage cabinet. He selected a double barreled Boss shotgun, took some shells, closed and locked the door, climbed up the basement stairs into the foyer. He loaded two shells, lowered the gun butt to the floor, leaned forward, pressed the twin barrels against his forehead and tripped both triggers. Write your version of Hemingway's suicide.

Ketchum Cemetery in Idaho

Hemingway is buried in this cemetery. Four tall pine trees shade his grave. He left a legacy of stories, poems, and personal letters. His homes in Oak Park, Illinois; Key West, Florida; Finca Vigia, Cuba; are museums. The Ketchum home is owned by the Nature Conservancy. Public tours are not offered.

Hemingway was larger than life. During the Hemingway Centennial celebration held at the John. F. Kennedy Library in Boston, essayist Joan Didion said of Hemingway, "This was a writer who had in his time made the English language new, changed the rhythms of the way both his own and the next few generations would speak and write and think."

About the author

Cathy is the author of two cookbooks. She lives in Auburn, Ca. with her husband, Ken, and little dog, Sophie.

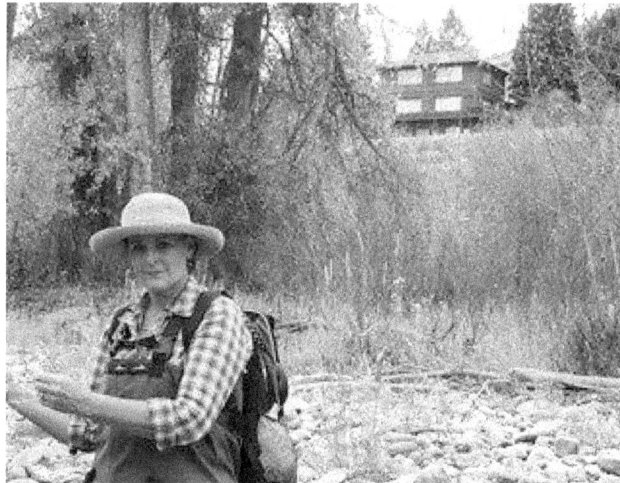

Fishing the Big Wood River in front of Hemingway's Ketchum home in 2015.

A special *Thank You* to my husband, Ken, for your
everlasting support and sharing my journey.

www.ingramcontent.com/pod-product-compliance
Lightning Source LLC
Chambersburg PA
CBHW062101090426
42741CB00015B/3300